SEABEE

SEABEES
"CAN DO!"

The United States Navy

The WWII War-Time Service Career
of Wendell S. Anderson

September 1943 thru October 1946

the Peppertree Press
Sarasota, Florida

Copyright ...*By No Means*

Any and all parts of this book are FREE to your use!
You may copy, record and use 'copy' and 'photo's' as you please.
Any and all data between the covers of this book need NO
PERMISSION from me the Author nor his Publisher
For your electronic recording, projection, copy and
Printing of the material of this book, *SEABEE*.

The Author, Wendell S. Anderson paid his dues, being proud
to serve his country and a career in the military of his
Country, THE UNITED STATES OF AMERICA

Andy's service time of combat of WWII was in service
of the Seabees and served under the command of
General Douglas MacArthur in our forces
Returning to the Philipines in 1944.

My hand and signature hereby grants release of all material of
copy and layout and photos of this book for the purchaser's
personal use and treatment as he wishes, and no date of
expiration.

Wendell S. Anderson

Andy

the Peppertree Press

Published by the Peppertree Press, LLC. the Peppertree Press and associated
logos are trademarks of the Peppertree Press, LLC.

For information call 941-922-2662 or contact us at our website: www.
peppertreepublishing.com or write to:
the Peppertree Press, LLC. Attention: Publisher
1269 First Street, Suite 7
Sarasota, Florida 34236

ISBN: 978-1-61493-180-5
Library of Congress Number: 2013907459
Printed in the U.S.A.
Printed May 2013

QUOTE: "I SHALL RETURN" General Mac Arthur 1942 ....
That we did in October 1944!

...THE STORIES AND PHOTOS, (WITHIN) WERE
COLLECTED AND PRESERVED FOR THESE NUMBER
OF YEARS, AND EVEN FOLLOWING THIS VETERAN
TO HIS RETIREMENT IN FLORIDA IN 1990. IT WAS SOME
SIXTY YEARS AGO THIS VETERAN, SERVING WITH
THE NAVAL SEABEES, FOUND THE PHILIPPINES HIS
HOME FOR A COUPLE OF YEARS. IT IS ONLY WITHIN
THESE RETIREMENT YEARS HAS 'ANDY' WENDELL
ANDERSON FOUND THE TIME TO PUT HIS COLLECTION
TOGETHER IN SOME SORT OF ORDER AND FASHION
THAT WOULD PRESERVE HIS EXPERIENCES IN A BOOK
FORMAT! PLEASE ENJOY OR STUDY THESE PHOTOS
AND ITEMS OF 'CAPTURE' SO AS YOU TOO AND YOU
YOUNGER FELLOWS CAN FOLLOW ONE 'BOYS'
WAR-TIME HISTORY!

WORLD WAR II 1941-1945

In gratitude for your war-time service

This certifies that

Wendell S. Anderson

upon meeting the strict requirements set forth by the

Congress of the United States of America

shall thereby be accepted for

Official Membership in

The American Legion

SERVED
1943
THRU
1946

VETERANS OF FOREIGN WARS
OF THE UNITED STATES
Recognizes

Mr Wendell S Anderson

for faithful support of America's deserving veterans and their families.

Patriotic Americans like you ensure that our nation remains
"the land of the free, and the home of the brave" for generations to come.

Allen "Gunner" Kent
Allen "Gunner" Kent
Adjutant General, Veterans of Foreign Wars

January 12, 2009
Date

I Served in
The United States Navy

Beach Boy—Philippines 1944   *Beach Boy—Sarasota 2011*

THE DAILY HAWK-EYE GAZETTE EXTRA

A BETTER NEWSPAPER

VOL. 9, NO. 140.   ASSOCIATED PRESS LEASED WIRE / UNITED PRESS LEASED WIRE   BURLINGTON, IOWA, SUNDAY, DECEMBER 7, 1941   MEMBER AUDIT BUREAU OF CIRCULATIONS / MEMBER IOWA DAILY PRESS ASSOCIATION   PRICE—5¢.

JAPANESE ATTACK
U. S., DECLARE WAR

SEVEN KNOWN DEAD IN ATTACK

Honolulu—(A.P.)—Japanese bombs killed at least seven persons and injured many others, three seriously, in a surprise morning aerial attack on Honolulu today.

Army officials announced that two Japanese planes had been shot down in the Honolulu area.

The dead, not immediately identified, included three Caucasians, two Japanese and a 10-year-old Portuguese girl.

Several fires were started in the city area, but all were immediately controlled.

EMERGENCY PROCLAIMED

Gov. Joseph B. Poindexter proclaimed M day emergency defense measures immediately in effect. He appointed Edward Doty in charge of the major disaster council.

The M-day proclamation established civilian-military control of traffic and roads, and permits the governor to issue food ration regulations.

First reports said 10 or more persons were injured when enemy planes sprayed bullets on the streets of Wahiawa, a town of around 3,000 population, about 20 miles northwest of Honolulu.

This report indicated the aerial attack was aimed at points on the island of Oahu other than Honolulu and the heavily fortified Pearl Harbor naval base.

DIE IS CAST, WILL DEFEND OUR COUNTRY

Local Citizens See Solid Backing for Govt. in War Crisis

Bitter resentment against Japan swept Burlington this afternoon as grim wires and radio brought news that Japan had declared war on the United States after without warning bomber attacks on Pearl Harbor, the city of Honolulu and against Manila, which caused destruction.

Hundreds of telephone calls poured into the office of the Hawk-Eye Gazette where up-to-the minute news was carried by the Associated Press. Other hundreds of people had come "down" for radios.

All other topics of conversation were pushed into the background. War had been declared against the United States.

There may have been a division

ARE WE EQUAL?   CHALLENGE?

Japan declared war following a sudden and anxious planes of our greatness at Pearl Harbor.

There followed attack of the Hawaiian islands of the Philippines.

Naval engagements

RADIO REPORT OF AIR ATTACK

New York, Dec. 7—(P)—Japanese warplanes killed 350 men at Hickam field and set fire to the U.S. battleship Oklahoma today in a sudden raid on Pearl Harbor and Honolulu, an NBC observer radioed direct from the scene today.

Several of the attacking planes, which came from the south, were shot down, he said.

In addition to these casualties from an air raid by planes which the observer identified as Japanese, he said three U.S. ships including the battleship Oklahoma, were affected in Pearl harbor.

RAID UNEXPECTED

The observer, standing on the roof of the Advertiser building in Honolulu, said the planes, undoubtedly Japanese, made the raid apparently. His report was suddenly broken off.

"We have witnessed this terrible air attack on Pearl Harbor and a severe bombing of Pearl Harbor by enemy planes, undoubtedly Japanese.

"The city of Honolulu has also been attacked and considerable damage done.

"This battle has been going on

United States today ng bombing by Japanese at Pearl Harbor.

nolulu, principal city huge Manila, capital

acific were reported

Washington — (AP)—Japan declared war upon the United States today. An electrified nation immediately united for a terrific struggle ahead. President Roosevelt was expected to ask congress for a declaration of war tomorrow.

During the day, Japanese planes bombed Honolulu, Pearl Harbor, and Hickam field, Hawaii, without warning. In a broadcast from Honolulu, some 350 soldiers were reported dead at Hickam field, with numerous casualties at the other points of attack.

Reports from Honolulu said there had been a ten engagement there.

At first the White House announced that Manila also had been bombed. But the Associated Press correspondent there reported at 3:25 p. m. central standard time, that all was quiet. The White House later said it had been unable to get substantiating reports of this attack on the Philippine capital and that President Roosevelt hoped the report of the bombing "at least is erroneous."

Shortly after the Hawaiian bombings became known, the Tokio government announced that Japan had entered a state of war with the United States and Great Britain as of 6 a. m. tomorrow (Monday).

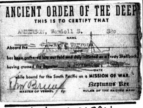

... WE HAD TO CARRY OUR 'UNION' CARDS TO WAR ...

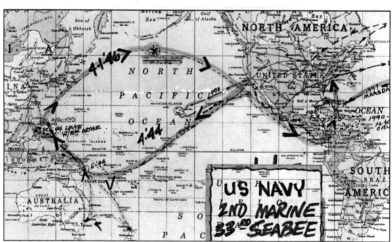

WWII Seabee Warrior

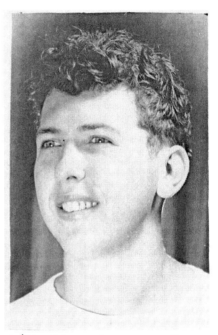

18 · WWII 1943 · NAVAL SEABEE ·

WENDELL S ANDERSON
HIGH SCHOOL KID AT 17 1942

...AT HOME FOR
SHORT LEAVE

AT THE 'OFFICE'

'MOTHER'S BOY'
TO SOUTH PACIFIC 2/44

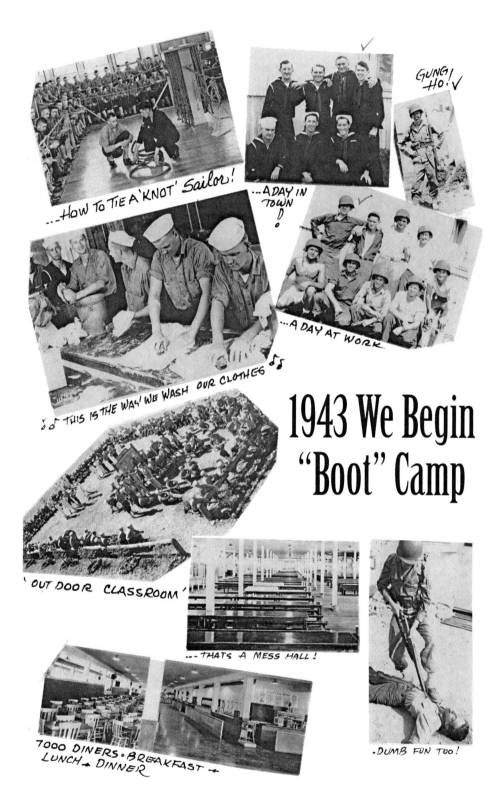

GUNG!
HO! ✓

...HOW TO TIE A 'KNOT' Sailor!

...A DAY IN TOWN

♪♪ THIS IS THE WAY WE WASH OUR CLOTHES ♪♪

...A DAY AT WORK

1943 We Begin "Boot" Camp

'OUT DOOR CLASSROOM'

...THATS A MESS HALL!

7000 DINERS • BREAKFAST • LUNCH • DINNER

.DUMB FUN TOO!

Summer 1944 "Ship Out" To the South Pacific

The Ship; HMS TORRENS (picture, to right) The photo is the only picture of our 80 day home that survived all the moves. The US NAVY commandeered this vessel of NORWAY because it was under the command of Hitler. The US NAVY performed a bit of conversion that we SEABEES could 'float the boat' to the South Pacific of our thousand men and all our construction equipment. We were out to sea and headed straight south (taking the long way around to the South Pacific. We loaded this ship with every item imaginable for living on another planet! We had trucks, hammers, nails, lumber, bandaids, cooking pot and pans, even the stoves,and also all the items necessary to establish a Field Hospital! Yes, the converted freighter was loaded for us to build our own village. We set sail out of OXNARD, California with destination unknown. We passengers were not privileged to 'Travel Plans'! We learned to navigate by starlight. We never had any lights on deck and also' Zig-Zagged'an

1941 MV HIGH SCHOOL SWEETHEART 'DEAR JOHN' FOLLOWED ...OUT TO SEA!

RUTH JENSKY

evasive measure to avoid contact with any enemy sub that may be hunting bait out there! The TORRENS was a slave ship including the torture chambers. No exhaust or circulating fans on this ship, and sleeping was impossible in the provided space for a canvas cot and supported by steel poles and bunking four high! A few of us washed our shirts and trousers by tying a line around our clothes and lowering them over the side and let the items drag along side for a salt water rinse!, (it gave us something to do). The first stop this old freighter

HMS TORRENS NORWAY FLAG

...PORT SIDE ACTION
NOTE: BOMB MISS FLACK

..STAR BOARD 'HITS'
'ZERO' TO A BATH

BROAD SIDE 'HIT'

THE 'LULL' UNTIL TOMORROW! 9

made, must have been 30 days out of California. We dropped anchor off GUADACANAL. A couple of our Supply officers went ashore 'scouting' for food supplies. They were able to get a number of cases of C rations... yuk! We must have received orders to continue on to the southern tip of NEW GUINEA, MELONIE BAY. A couple of months at this location, and we received orders to 'reload' our freighter and head north to

NEPTUNE'S REX

HOLLANDIA, NEW GUINEA. Rumor had it, that the 33rd SEABEE outfit would be preparing for a run to the PHILIPPINES. Another 30 day wait, and finally our ship joined a formation of ships in Convoy! The pictures below tried to capture events of our convoy being attacked all the way to the Philippines!

1944 WWII

SAMAR PHILIPPINE FAMILY

GRANDMA AT 44

ANTIQUE WWII V-MAIL

OH YES — SENT THIS ONE HOME!

BATTLE OF LEYTE GULF

Our battle of LEYTE generally considered to be the largest Naval Battle of World War II, and by some criteria, possibly the largest Naval Battle in history.

Off shore of LEYTE and in the Straits of Luzon, Mindano and Samar on the North Side was the battle scene. This was October of 1944 … the Admirals; HALSEY, KINKAID and MITSCHER engaged the Imperial JAPANESE NAVY in masterful combat, proving disastrous for the Japanese Fleet.

The Battle of SIBUYAN SEA, SURIGAO STRAIT, CAPE ENGANO and the SAMAR BATTLE laid waste to most of Japan's 'Heavies'. Many of their fleet 'limped' back to Japan licking their wounds. Major repairs were intended upon many of the ships of their fleet. Most of those ships never returned to active service to fight again.

When we learned of our results of this deciding battle we felt much at ease. Late October 1944 was indeed our turning point of our SOUTH PACIFIC engagement with the Japanese Navy!

We noticed that our military in the invading return to the Philippines did not mime the NORMANDY OFFENSIVE that our Military and the British Armies formatted for the Europe invasion.

Our Construction Battalion was able to 'turn-to' and build our Camp site, constructed Docks for all the Liberty Ships standing by with tons of materials for our 7th Fleet Naval Base of SAMAR.

Ref: maps of the invasion Battles Pages 22 & 23.

SPANIARD MAGELLAN DIRECTED THE CONSTRUCTION OF THIS CHURCH IN 1782

DOWNTOWN GUIUAN, SAMAR

MY NEIGHOR'S HOME

MY HOME 1944

OCEAN
VIEW
→

UPPER CLASS LAND OWNER

→
BUILD
THE
ROOF
FIRST
—
SHADE
FOR
THE
REST
OF
PROJECT

GREAT NEIGHBORS'
TOWN HOUSE
(2) STORY

GUIUAN 'DOWN-TOWN'
MERCHANTS AND LOGAN

...WE ALL HAO GREAT
UNIFORMS

...WE BUILT A
BRIDGE

KIDS AT THEIR
COMMUNITY TOILET

← THE NEIGHBORS

'GOLD COAST'

HOLLANDIA, NEW GUINEA

It was OCTOBER 1944 our ship, The HMS TORRENS was given orders to 'hoist anchor' and join in Convoy some 30 to 40 ships that have been riding anchor in the harbor of Hollandia the past month! The ship TORRENS flew a NORWEGIAN flag. Her gun crew was removing canvas covers, oiling breaches and cleaning their cannon's barrels.

Our 33rd SEABEE BATTALION of 1000 men and all their equipment were aboard. This ship we have had to call home since leaving the States some 90 days prior. We were all very bored of our life style as the ship offered NO COMFORTS! The steel decks were hot enough to fry a couple of eggs. We were anchored in Hollandia Bay and that is located on the Equator/HOT.

Our troops didn't need a newspaper to tell us we are headed into harms-way. "Where are we headed now?" The voices sounding from the very bored SEABEES!

It took a couple of days for all those ships to gather off NEW GUINEA to form Convoy formation. Positioning those ships called for lots of 'flag' and signal light messaging from ship to ship and to shore.

Communications between Admirals and Skippers; one could hear the ascendancy among command!

We 'uninformed' lot had no idea of the fierce battles that our allied fleets were engaged in and around those PHILIPPINE ISLANDS! In our world of all Naval Battles none surpassed the size and numbers of warships engaged as was the LEYTE-SAMAR STRAITS BATTLE: some 12 Battleships, 20

MORE GOLD COAST

or so Carriers, 50-60 Destroyers and numbers of other combatant vessels made up the combined ships of JAPAN and the US NAVY that were engaged in this mighty of all Sea Battles! So many ships were Sunk, so many received damages that were beyond their combat readiness, and the Japanese receiving near total defeat that many ships had to escape at night and 'limp' back to Japan to lick wounds and get repairs. Naval History tells me those Navies engaged in the largest Sea Battle ever recorded in our History of Sea Warfare.

After the Battle had subsided our Convoy was ordered to the LEYTE-SAMAR BAY. We were just a few hours out of NEW GUINEA and the land based Jap Zeros found our Convoy.

Our Convoy guns fought off Zeros all the way to the Philippines 5-6 days. Yes we lost some ships too!

The village of TACLOBAN, PHILIPPINES was our destination. We would be meeting the Mac ARTHUR assemblage and all his aids for the 'famous' picture shoot of the General's return to the Philippines!

Four Decades later I found and give my due to the US NAVY for all the work they did in 'clearing' our path to safety, for our landing in the Philippines. I owe much gratitude to those Admirals and sailors of our 3rd and 7th fleet,

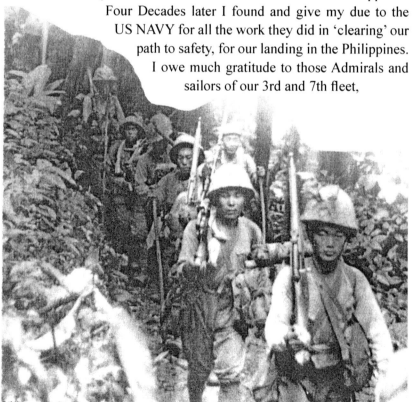

The JAPANESE introduced a most lethal weapon at this stage in their war with the USA. Our Convoy was introduced to the KAMIKAZE PILOT. Our Baptism to WAR came to our Convoy via the KAMIKAZE PILOT!

"HERE HE COMES!" We shouted from the shade of our ship's Gun Tower. Pointing to the direction of a Zero skimming along the water's surface and threading his way around the ships of our Starboard Flank and he was Targeting us! Our Norwegian gunner 'times' his shell, loaded his shell into the Cannon's breach and FIRES! SCORE! we all

shouted! That KAMIKAZE had us in his sights. Our ship was not a warship! Had the gunner missed his 'one' shot the TORRENS would be sitting at the bottom of the Mariana Trench (The deepest known bottom of our oceans of our world!

THE BATTLE FOR
LEYTE GULF

By Admiral Thomas C. Kinkaid, USN and Admiral Marc A. Mitscher, USN

IT WAS between 23 and 26 October, 1944, that the Jap made his great challenge to our landings in the Philippines. During that period major naval and air actions occurred, actions that involved our carriers and battleships, cruisers and destroyers, submarines and PT boats.

There were three enemy forces to be dealt with. The first of these included 2 battleships, 1 heavy cruiser, and 4 destroyers. This force approached Leyte through Surigao Strait, and on the night of 24-25 October came into contact with units of our Seventh Fleet. In anticipation of the enemy's arrival, the Seventh Fleet was deployed in and at the mouth of the strait, so that when the Japanese had steamed into the trap they found themselves in the stem of a "T" crossed by

American cruisers and battleships, and flanked by light forces. In naval terminology, to be the stem of a "T" is to be caught in a hopeless position. Our heavy units pounded the dismayed Japs with big guns while destroyers launched fierce torpedo attacks. It was grim irony for the Japs. They were being sunk that night by our old battleships that they had "destroyed" at Pearl Harbor. The outcome of that encounter was decisive. Only one enemy destroyer escaped to meet defeat again. Only one of our ships, a destroyer, sustained damage.

While the enemy's Southern Force was being destroyed, the second force, to be known as the Central Force, was passing through San Bernardino Strait. Already it had been reduced in size, but still it came on.

On the 23rd two of our submarines had intercepted this force off Palawan when it consisted of 5 battleships, 10 heavy cruisers, 1 or 2 light cruisers, and about 15 destroyers. Our subs attacked and sank 2 heavy cruisers and seriously damaged another.

THE CENTRAL FORCE

ON THE 24th the Third Fleet carriers struck the Central Force as it passed through Mindoro Strait. Our carrier planes sent the Jap's new battleship *Musashi*, 1 cruiser, and 1 destroyer to the bottom. Other units were badly mauled. Yet despite these losses, the Japanese Central Force continued its drive for Leyte Gulf.

That same afternoon, carrier planes from our Third Fleet sighted the third, or Northern, enemy force north of Luzon. It was decided that our fast carrier task groups should intercept this force, and so, that night we steamed northward.

Dawn found the enemy's Central Force coming through San Bernardino Strait and down upon the 7th Fleet escort carriers and screens which were in three groups off Samar. An engagement followed with this enemy, at that time composed of 4 battleships, 5 cruisers, and 11 destroyers. Our lightly armed carriers retired, striking back at this formidable enemy with unexcelled courage. After more than two and one-half hours of struggle the enemy broke off the engagement, and withdrew in the direction of San Bernardino Strait.

Planes of the escort carriers and the Third Fleet struck the Central Force that afternoon, sinking 2 enemy heavy cruisers and 1 destroyer. Again on the 26th our planes attacked the depleted force and inflicted severe damage that resulted in several sinkings. Our losses in action with the Central Force amounted to one escort carrier and 2 destroyers sunk by surface fire, and approximately 105 planes.

That same morning to the north our Third Fleet commenced launching air attacks, and continued striking the Northern Force until 1800 that evening. By the end of the day this enemy force of 1 large carrier, 3 light carriers, 2 battleships with flight decks, 5 cruisers, and 6 destroyers was but a ghost. It was a "fleet out of being."

Forty of our planes went down in combat, and the light carrier *Princeton* was our only unit lost. The day was ours. The enemy fleet that had hoped to turn us back at Leyte had been cut to ribbons. Those enemy ships that were able to do so put on all possible steam for the homeland, and our reconquest of the Philippines went ahead.

T. C. Kinkaid

Marc Mitscher

Battle of Leyte Gulf

Part of the Pacific War, World War II

We passed a 'liner' to a steel helmet collecting money as one would do passing the plate in church! That gunner saved a lot of lives on our ship that day, he received over $700. US dollars! Thanks to another unknown fellow of my War!

Finally, our Convoy drops anchor in the Bay of Leyte. We made it! Now we began thinking in anticipation as to what the coming days would bring. We know the fears of War now, we have heard the cannons firing in anger as well as the screaming of an enemies plane and releasing his bomb on a target of Sea or Land! Small power boats were Taxiing officers and messengers about the bay, ship to shore or ship to ship. We learned that former Japanese occupiers of Leyte are now hiding low, as their ammo and supply ships were possibly sunk during the previous days of fending off the enemy from coming to the Leyte area!

THANKS AGAIN US NAVY for making waste of defending the entire area for our safe arrival!

Years later of the 1944 events of the Philippines my research, informed me, ADMIRALS: Halsey, Kinkaid, and Mitscher were so successful in mastering the seas in this vital landing area of LEYTE-SAMAR.

In a few days came DECEMBER 5, 1944 a day when all available forces of JAPANESE were assigned mission to RETAKE LEYTE! They must have mustered all available fighters to RETAKE LAYTE. All combat missions by the Japs seemingly, always came at dawn and at sunset! Three (3) DC2s flew in low over our 'under construction' airfield. Someone yells, 'Whopee" we haven't had mail for months, here comes the 'mail planes' 'WRONG!' ... we learned later that JAPAN ordered and bought the DC2 from

Douglas Aircraft Industries prior to Pearl Harbor. Douglas made model changes to the DC2 and sold the product line DC3to the US AIRFORCE as well as commercial Air Lines for use as commercial

Second battle of Philippines Sea, the Battle for Leyte Gulf

aircraft for the industry of the USA. The DC2s made a circle as if to file a landing pattern, WOOPS....OUT JUMPED JAP PARATROOPS! We scattered, no guns in hand. Those Troops were annihilated within a couple of hours of a fire fight with our Marine Squads. The Army wascamped across the unfinished air-field. They kept coming across the field (dark now) and met with our guys ...as friendly forces, thinking we were enemy. The Japs has torched a couple of our Piper Cub scout planes, that was their only success to equipment damage. I heard calls to "STOP DAM IT!" action was slow to wind down. A number of our US ARMY were injured as well as some fatals. Mistakes of War! This long Story made Short, MAC ARTHUR ORDERED ALL NAVY AND MARINES OFF LEYTE IN THE MORNING!

That was indeed a sorrowful night...a badly confused night as well as deadly! We SEABEES and MARINES were ordered off LEYTE, and instructed to move across the bay to SAMAR, PHILIPPINES.

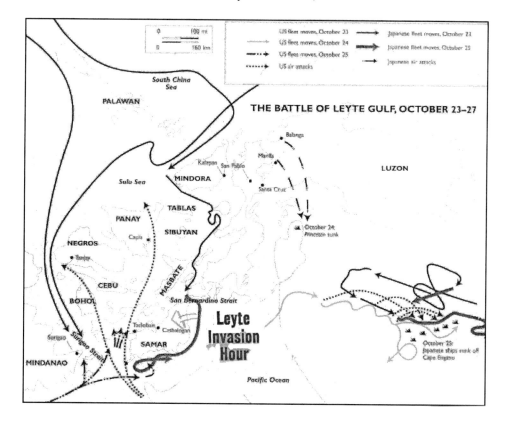

THE BATTLE OF LEYTE GULF, OCTOBER 23–27

THE LAST DAYS OF

THE JAPANESE FLEET

By Rear Admiral Robert B. Carney, USN

WITH the overwhelming defeat of the main Imperial Japanese Battle Fleet at the battles of the Philippine Sea and Leyte Gulf, the remnants of the Japanese forces sought the comparative safety of their home bases. The job of destroying or neutralizing the moderately powerful task force that remained from the once proud Japanese fleet was given to the United States Fleet's fast carrier forces.

On 14 March 1945, the carrier force proceeded toward Japan proper to seek out and destroy those Japanese units based on the home island of Kyushu. This was to be the first of many strikes at the home islands planned as a measure to divert attention, and naval and air strength, from the Okinawa invasion.

The first strike met with signal success. Besides the destruction of air fields and installations in the Kure-Kobe area, the carrier based planes heavily damaged the Japanese carrier *Ryuho*, tied up at Kure.

SUPPORT OF OKINAWA

WHEN the invasion of Okinawa began on 1 April, planes from the fast carriers began a series of almost continuous strikes and combat patrols in direct support of the operation. For the first few days enemy air activity was light, but on 6 April, the Japanese struck with full force. After beating off the savage enemy air attacks, the carrier force turned northward, and on 7 April, located a task force of the remaining Japanese fleet. In spite of heavy weather and violent anti-aircraft fire, carrier planes attacked and sank the Japanese super-battleship *Yamato*, the cruiser *Yahagi*, and four escorting destroyers. In thirty minutes of violent precision bombing and torpedo attacks, the suicidal sally of the Jap force had been broken at a cost to us of seven planes.

With the victorious end of the Okinawa operation, the Navy offensive against the Japanese homeland mounted in intensity. Combining deception and relentless pressure, the Third Fleet carrier and surface forces pounded the Empire.

On 24, 25, and 28 July, in a series of U. S. Navy carrier strikes unparalleled in modern history, the remainder of the Japanese fleet was sunk or severely damaged in raids on the Kure Naval Base. In these strikes the battleships *Haruna*, *Hyuga*, and *Ise*, all damaged in previous attacks, were sunk. Also sunk or heavily damaged were the carrier *Katsuragi*, the heavy cruisers *Aoba* and *Tone*, the light cruisers *Oyodo* and *Kitagami*, and a number of destroyers and minor combatant ships.

THE LAST OF THE JAPS

THIS strike completed the job of neutralizing the Japanese fleet and the job was the U. S. Navy's answer to Pearl Harbor. At the time of the surrender of the Japanese forces the only combatant ships of the Japanese fleet left afloat and undamaged were the cruiser *Sakawa* and a handful of destroyers and submarines.

Also afloat, but heavily damaged, were the battleship *Nagato*, three light cruisers, and three light or converted carriers.

Japanese losses during the war included 12 battleships, 15 carriers, 4 escort carriers, 15 heavy cruisers, 1 old heavy cruiser, 20 light cruisers, 126 destroyers, and 125 submarines.

But the Nip Navy was not the only target. Our surface groups bombarded the coast wherever good targets could be found; steel mills were demolished by 16″ shells, car ferries and fishing fleets were sunk, locomotives were destroyed and industries wrecked. The bombardments brought home to millions of Japs the fact that they were powerless to stop us and were doomed.

No single factor contributed more than the bombardments in informing the Japanese people of the truth so long held from them—that the war was lost.

And mark you! Japan sued for peace before the atomic bomb hit Hiroshima and before Russia entered the Pacific war.

▶ The Japanese carrier **Zuiho** under attack during the battle off Cape Engano on October 25.

KEY PERSONALITIES

ADMIRAL HALSEY

Admiral William Frederick Halsey (1882–1959), an expert in the use of destroyers in the early 1930s, was attracted to the new technology and theory surrounding naval airpower during the prewar years. Indeed in 1935, at the age of 52, he qualified as a pilot. He became one of the US Navy's most talented air power commanders, and was in command of the US Pacific Fleet's airpower when war broke out. In the difficult early months of the war, his aggressive counterstrikes, including the Doolittle Raid on April 18, 1942, led the press to nickname him "Bull" Halsey. Though he missed the Battle of Midway through ill health, he was given tactical command in the south Pacific in 1943, specifically to give more belligerence to the efforts of the naval leadership. As much as his bravery and belligerence was appreciated by the common soldier, his aggressive tendencies occasionally led him to run dangerous risks – most notably at the Battle of Leyte Gulf. His penchant for attacking the Japanese whenever possible caused him to fall for the Japanese attempt to lure him away from protecting MacArthur's men landing on Leyte. Had it not have been for mistakes on the Japanese side, then total disaster could have befallen the US forces because of his actions. Nonetheless, he alternated command of the Pacific Fleet with Admiral Spruance until the end of the war.

OCTOBER 25

SEA WAR, *LEYTE GULF*

US Task Force 38 heads northwards to intercept Ozawa's carrier force, believing the Japanese Centre and Southern Forces to be in retreat. However,

OCTOBER 26

SEA WAR, *LEYTE GULF*

The Battle of Leyte Gulf ends in a massive US victory. Several more Japanese cruisers and destroyers are sunk today by pursuing US aircraft. The final tally of Japanese shipping sunk is four aircraft carriers, three battleships, ten cruisers, eleven destroyers and one submarine, with most other Japanese ships severely damaged. In addition, 10,000 sailors and 500 aircraft are also lost. The Battle of Leyte Gulf marks the undeniable collapse of Japanese naval power in the Pacific. From this point on, the suicide air strikes that had their inauguration over Leyte Gulf become an increasing feature of a desperate Japanese military that can no longer oppose the mighty US Navy.

Drawn by: (self) WENDELL ANDERSON   'MAC IS BACK!' October 1944

THERE WERE ALWAYS SHIPS AWAITING DOCK SPACE –

THE VESSELS ABOVE ARE LCIs LANDING CRAFT INFANTRY ... OUTFITTING FOR JAPAN

WE BUILT A MAJOR
PORT AT GUIUAN FOR
HALSEY'S 7TH FLEET
DOCKS WERE
BUILT FOR WAR SUPPLIES
NEEDED FOR THE MOVE
TO JAPAN

A DRY DOCK WAS MOVED
IN FOR SHIP REPAIR
A MAJOR
REPAIR YARD
FOR OUR FLEET

_NOTE HOW LOW THE
SHIPS WERE ALONG THE
DOCKS _ ALL SHIPS COMING
TO THE WAR ZONE WERE
LOADED TO THE 'GUNNELS'
_OUR STEVEADORS
UNLOAD THEM AND SEND
THEM BACK TO
USA

_WHEN THE WAR WAS
OVER _ ABOUT 20 OF US GOT
ON AN 'AK' FOR TRIP BACK HOME
IN MARCH OF 1946. WE WERE
GRANTED PASSAGE BACK TO THE
STATES _TRAVERSING THE
PANAMA CANAL TO NORFOLK V/A
30 DAY'S AT SEA (TO THE STATES)!

_ _ _A CRUISER CAME BY_ _

(ABOVE) 'BABY' AIR CRAFT CARRIER CAME TO SAMAR
WITH A COUPLE OF SQUADRONS OF NEW
CORSAIRS FOR OUR 'MAG' OUTFITS (MARINE)
PILOTS. THE HULL OF A VICTORY SHIP WAS
FITTED WITH A 'PARKING LOT' FOR THE FULL
LOAD OF NEW AIRPLANES!

...WHEN WE
WERE IN CONVOY
FROM NEW GUINEA
← A LIKE GUN
AND 'GUNNER'
SCORED A 'HIT'
OF A JAP PLANE
SAVING US!

A 'SCOW' FREIGHTER WAS
MY TROOP SHIP

1000 MEN CAME TO THE SOUTH
PACIFIC WITH OUR BULL DOZERS

KILROY WAS HERE

SAMAR PAINT CO
BOYD & TALBOT

"COME ON GUYS _ WE'RE GOING TO SEE
A MOVIE TONIGHT"_ YOU KNOW WE DID!

'TALBOTT'& HIS PAINT SHOP....HE WAS
INSTRUCTED BY CHAPLIN TO DRESS
LADY(ABOVE)... "SHUCKS"

"HOW LONG DO I HAVE TO WAIT?"

....."HEY MAC ARE YOU 21?" NO
BEER WITHOUT YOUR MOMMY'S
PERMISSION!

TOOLS

..."HOW YOU PAYING _ VISA OR CASH"

...WE HAD THE BEST BARBER SHOP IN S.P.

MY COMMANDING OFFICER

SO THE 33RD BUILT ITS' OWN LUTHERN AND... OR BAPTIST CHURCH 1945

RIGGING SHOP • CABLE FOR UN-LOADING SHIPS.

THE 61ST BUILT THEIR CHAPPEL TOO!

SPANISH INFLUENCE...THIS CHURCH
GUIUAN, SAMAR

IT WAS SAID THAT SPANISH EXPLORER MAGELLAN
CONTRIBUTED TO THE DESIGN AND CONSTRUCTION
OF THIS CHURCH AT GUIUAN,SAMAR

A)

B)

A) PICTURE AND **B)** picture exposed
My location in the PHILIPPINES. My mother discovered the picture
In a religious magazine in Chicago...She had just received the identical
Photo (censored) from me of the Parrish ladies.   She wrote back, "You
Must be on the island of SAMAR in the PHILIPPINES!"

MAGELLAN WAS HERE IN 1782

"THE WHITE WASH PAINT WAS SOME
SEA BEE OFFICER'S ORDER!"

THE WAR MADE BELIEVERS OF US ALL! †

...LITTLE SAND ON
OUR BEACH!

MAYFLOWER VAN LINES !!

RAZOR SHARP
BEACH! ...'CORAL'

...OUR NEW MOVIE HOUSE!

TONY & BOB 'RENTED' OUR
VAN FROM U-HAUL!

JUST NEIGHBORS

TENT CITY... RAIN RAIN RAIN...

GREAT 'DUCK' POND

PHILIPPINO LIVE BY THE SEA

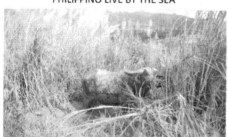

FRIENDLY NEIGHBOR

...WE BORROWED A COUPLE OF 'BOMBS'
FROM THE AIR FORCE...INSTANT SWIMMING
POOL OUT ON THE REEF...HOT WATER POOL TOO!

SORRY__NO COLOR PHOTOS — 1944

MIAMI BEACH! NEED I EXPLAIN?

ISLAND 'VIKINGS' FOUND $'s...US SAILORS

OUR TRAILER PARK OF PAST
6 MONTHS!
We procured a delightful
'ritzy' subdivision for
Our 33RD SEABEE
BATTALION
GUIUAN, SAMAR

--- THE NEW SIDE STREETS WILL BE PALM LINED STREETS /

NOTE: STANDING WATER 'MONSOONS' PROMPTED OUR NEW CAMP 'GATED' COMMUNITY!

FALL OF 1944

NO RUNNING WATER 'BUT CLASS'

OUR WRIGLEY FIELD

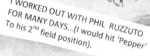

I WORKED OUT WITH PHIL RUZZUTO FOR MANY DAYS...(I would hit 'Pepper' To his 2nd field position).

SOUTH PACIFIC 'RITZ'

5th BOMB GROUP'S STORAGE YARD!

WE CALLED IT A 'GRUG' FENCE

— WE EVEN BUILT A HOSPITAL 'OUT BY 3RD BASE! SPRING 1945

KILROY WAS HERE TOO

CORSAIR

---YOU CAN'T FLY IT___YOU'RE COLOR BLIND !

...CONVOY 'HEADING' PHILIPPINES OCT. 1944

ALL ISLANDS LOOK ALIKE

'SICK BAY'

"NOW HEAR THIS"

...OUR SUBDIVSION ●SAMAR●

THE 33ᴿᴰ SPECIAL SEABEE BATTALION

SAMAR, PHILIPPINES
1944-1945

OUR 33ᴿᴰ SPECIAL BECAME
THE NON-UNION STEVEDORE
SHOP OF THE SOUTH PACIFIC

...OUR DINING HALL SERVED
1000 MEALS PER DAY.
CREWS WERE SERVED
BREAKFAST, LUNCH,DINNER
AND MIDNIGHT 'LUNCH'
OUR CREWS WERE
ON THE JOB
24 HOURS 7DAY P/ WEEK

'UNIFORMS WERE,
ONE OF A KIND'

"our 33ʳᵈ turns a ship
Around in less than
12 hours!"
This 33ʳᵈ also holds all
Records ... 700 barrels of
Fuel (UNLOADED) in less than
12 HOURS!
THAT'S THE 1944-45 FEAT!

FORMAL ATTIRE • DINING ROOM

FREE MOVIE TOMORROW NIGHT

DISCUSSING
LADIES BACK HOME

WENDELL S. ANDERSON

FOR YOUR INTEREST, The following is a short 'BIO' of this lad Of 17 years, joining the US NAVY granted by his MOMMY'S Permission ONLY!

... $\mathbf{H}$ow can a WWII war veteran write his war career of nearly 4 years in a short paragraph or two? However here is this Swede's story!

At the age of 17 enlisted in the US NAVY (with mommys' permission) This was 1943. I wanted to be a Naval Pilot! 'Physical Exam day: proved this Kid, Colorblind. "You can't tell the difference from Red & Green!" Re: that's a port and/ or starboard lighting, you can't tell if a ship or aircraft is coming or going!" Too bad Sailor, but we will set you up in the

AT AGE 80

SEABEES... I asked what is a SEABEE? Naval Construction Battalions... Some bystander added, "Shock Troopers!" No reneging now...I was sworn in officially...US NAVY.

After some 'Boot' training etc., now 1944 Secretly, a Battalion of 1000 old men, and me the "KID" set out to sea...Heading South West Pacific, aboard an old freighter under a Norwegian Flag! Remember? Norway was not one of us in WWII. The ship, HMS TORRENS.

...about 30 days later we were camping out on a small Island across the Channel from Guadalcanal. Movie nite in the rain, squatting on my steel helmet watched a Hollywood movie, John Wayne's' FIGHTING SEABEES ...Now I learned the identity of a SEABEE...(I think)! We moved on to the Southern Tip of NEW GUINEA. ...Building our camp site in PALMOLIVE PEETS' Coconut Groves... Built some Docks, a hospital, and an air strip, Bush-Men of New Guinea helped us too!

AT AGE 50

Seemed like we just got ashore, and we received order to tear down our camp and reload our Norwegian ship! ...trucks, jeeps, tents, lumber, bulldozers and we old men! We headed up the Coast of New Guinea...Hollandia became our 'ship board' home for about a month! ....Wow, Hot on those Steel Decks, Why? Rumor has it we are waiting to form an Invasion Convoy .... That was a long wait indeed! End of September '44 we were underway....6 knot Convoy, North! A couple of days out, The Jap Zeros were coming out of the Sun and the Clouds (Jap pilot say, Sink the Convoy) ...That they almost did! ....All our ships (about 30) were busy firing all cannon as fast as they could reload! ...Smoke was coming from a couple of the ships and they were without power and fell out of the Convoy. This battle went on for a few days!, We must have looked like ducks sitting on a pond in the back 40 of the farm!

MAC ARTHUR wanted this Kid Seabee to aid him in his return to the PHILIPPINES! Our Convoy received a lot of hits those days! OCTOBER 44 was D Day for the US and Mac Arthur to return to the Philippines! Admiral Halsey, and our Air Forces Must have been doing a masterful job of blocking the Heavy Cannon from getting near us! The landing at Leyte Bay was nearly uneventful...most of the enemy took off for the hills upon seeing our arrival. We even had time to make a sign to welcome the 2nd division Marines ashore!...A few weeks later... December 5 all hell broke loose.,

The Japanese returned also...Mr. Moto must have assembled every ship and aircraft they could muster. I'm sure his orders were, "GET THAT GUY MAC ARTHUR AND HIS GI s' BACK TO SEA!" Their counter attack failed...Mac was back! ...However that fierce battle ended up with Confusion...Our Naval forces and Marines held position on one side of our unfinished air strip...The Army was on the other side. Jap paratroopers dropped on our strip, torched a couple of Piper Cubs (scout planes) and we were able to put all the parachutest out of commission, and by this time the Army thought we were the enemy. Many fatalities that night! CONFUSION AND ACTIVITY WAS RAMPANT!

It was the next day or so, when MAC ARTHUR ordered all Navy and Marines out of Leyte! We brought our ship around to the Island of SAMAR, anchoring out and we Were escorted ashore by the Naval Landing Craft. We established our new 'Beach-head' on SAMAR the village of Guiwan....We built a great Air Field for the Army's 13th AIR FORCE, and a number of Bomb Groups. We had the MAG outfits in and the NAVY'S SQUADRONS TOO! SO THE WAR WENT ON... Our bombers the 24s were busy with working all islands and Japanese bases and camps up north!

This lad was now almost an 'old man' 20 years, Our command was now the 2"1 Division Marines. We listened to TOKYO ROSBightly, she would give us State Side news such as "Who is Sleeping with your Wife tonite? Some of the 4F fellows are most likely taking care of your Home Life!" That gal ROSE knew how to get to the 'Old Boys of my outfit!

Finally, Our President HARRY TRUMAN ordered the Bomb to the Pacific Theatre... Realize Europe and Hitler were gone but this thing in the Pacific went on until the ABomb...Whew!... my outfit was suiting up for the Beach-head of JAPAN..."THANK YOU HARRY!" How lucky this Kid was!

The War with JAPAN was now over... We all had the points, "Let's get back to the States" that was August '45 ...I'm still studying my 'Jungle Rot' detailing the many camp sites, Many jeeps, trucks, bombs, ammo, junk junk ....loaded onto barges and pushed over-board into the Sea for disposal! A few of us young kids were the last to leave Samar... as I was on a 'Kiddy Hitch' (I had a few months in 1946 to fulfill my Enlistment time expiring in Oct of 1946).

DON'T LEAVE ME HERE! ...As I bid farewell to troop after troop!... Finally, March of 46 about 20 of us were able to get a ride and a Naval Ship going back to Norfolk, Virginia. Across the Pacific heading home! APRIL 1ST we encountered a savage wave in the North Pacific...This ship we were riding rode up and over a wave that would measure many stories tall...It was aTI DAL WAVE so fierce it swept many lads from their Quonset huts and their gun mounts of the ALASKA coast...That wave swept and killed many young children in Hawaii, all within the day of APRIL FIRST 1946,

Again we gave thanks to our Lord for bringing us threw that happening! ....I have now had enough of this 'crap' called WAR!

We now began our SEABEE work in earnest! Other SEABEE BATTALIONS came to SAMAR. Our Base became very large, our Airfield became official of the 13th AIRFORCE, MARINE AIR GROUPS, US FLEET aircraft were based at SAMAR. Our base grew fast and large, DOCKS, WAREHOUSES, ROADWAYS, HOSPITALS, DRY DOCKS FOR SHIP REPAIR, AND EVEN A RESORT FOR SAILOR R&R (Rest and Relaxation).

The NAVY and ARMY and MAC ARTHUR had their own Communities, as well as their own COMMAND!

The GENERALS and ADMIRALS were now becoming more confident of our war and its mobility!

WASHINGTON DC and President HARRY S. TRUMAN were feeling the strength of our forces, and the move for the JAPANESE home land was within reach and in the 'forefront' of War activities since the EUROPEAN WAR had been resolved!

We SEABEES and my 33rd BATTALION sensed our spot on the planning table for our participation on the Homeland of JAPAN. We asked our Supply Officer what is those crates of clothing doing at our doorstep, and also we notice crates of new rifle?

"WE KNEW THE REST OF THE STORY!"

...THANKS, HARRY S. TRUMAN

JAPAN SURRENDERS 1945

POTSDAM CONFERENCE. Germany's fate is decided at Potsdam by leaders of the victorious Allies. Other important decisions were made here also, including a declaration which paved the way for capitulation by Japan. UPPER. The conference opens in a room of the palace at Potsdam, Germany. LOWER. Wars and conferences on wars do not stop a democratic people from expressing their will at the ballot box, and a change of leaders does not disrupt an aroused people from prosecuting a common end. Death brought a new United States leader to the "Big Three;" and election gave Britain a new leader during the Potsdam conference. Here is shown the new "Big Three," Prime Minister Attlee, President Truman, and Marshall Stalin.

EMPEROR HIROHITO

THE JAPS ACCEPT SURRENDER—14 AUGUST 1945

PRESIDENT ANNOUNCES VICTORY. Tuesday, August 14, 1945, dawned clear and warm in Washington. Official and unofficial Washington spent a nervous day, listening, watching, waiting. When the marble columned office buildings were emptied, the streets filled rapidly; suburban gardens went untended; eating places filled beyond their normal capacity. Crowds began an early vigil in Lafayette Square, opposite the White House. News and radio correspondents were summoned at 6:45 to a White House Press Conference. At seven o'clock the President greeted reporters. In his hands was a message from the Swiss Legation; its contents were the Japanese diplomatic words accepting the terms of the Potsdam Declaration. War was over. Peace had come at last.

THE SURRENDER OF JAPAN

By Admiral of the Fleet William F. Halsey, USN

BY JULY, 1945, the United States Fleet had brought to bear in the Pacific tremendous sea-air power. Our carrier planes were blasting air fields, navy yards, industries, and storage facilities throughout the "home islands" of the Japanese Empire. Our battleships, cruisers, and destroyers bombarded the "sacred soil" of Nippon almost at will. Our submarines had ventured into the innermost parts of the Inland Sea and the Sea of Japan and had made those waters as unsafe for Japanese shipping as the waters of the Southwest Pacific and the China Sea.

As a prelude to the main and final objective, the invasion of Japan, the preliminary bombings and bombardments were stepped up. Our secret weapon, the atomic bomb, was used, first against the military targets and industries at Hiroshima. Later against the munitions plants and repair yards at Nagasaki. Our ally Russia entered the war in Manchuria; China, armed with lend-lease supplies, began new drives against the enemy.

THE JAPS ACCEPT SURRENDER

WHEN the Japanese delivered their message of acceptance of the Potsdam Ultimatum on 14 August, the Third Fleet was ready with plans for occupation, and the unprecedented operation was executed smoothly. The official instrument of surrender was presented to the Japanese representatives by General of the Army MacArthur at Manila on 19 August. This instrument provided for the capitulation of the Imperial General Staff, and the surrender of all ground, sea, and air commanders of the Islands of Japan, the Philippine Islands, and the Southern parts of Korea to the Commander-in-Chief, United States Army Forces, Pacific; the surrender of all land, sea, air, and auxiliary force commanders in the Japanese mandated islands was to be made to the Commander-in-Chief, United States Pacific Fleet.

The first units of the United States Third Fleet, after being delayed for two days by a typhoon, moved into Sagami Bay, southwest of Tokyo Bay, on 27 August in the first step of the occupation.

On 29 August, Fleet Admiral Nimitz arrived from Guam and boarded his flagship, the battleship South Dakota. Admiral Halsey, Commander of the Third Fleet, entered Tokyo Bay and anchored off Yokosuka Naval Base in the forenoon of that day. On 30 August, 10,000 Marines and Naval personnel landed on this base and the surrounding fortress islands. The naval base at Tateyama, across the bay from Yokosuka, was occupied on 1 September by Marine forces as the occupation control progressed smoothly and rapidly.

The formal surrender of the Imperial Japanese Government was made aboard the United States battleship Missouri in Tokyo Bay at 0908 on 2 September 1945. General of the Army MacArthur signed as Supreme Commander for the Allied Powers, and Fleet Admiral Nimitz as representative for the United States.

THE ISLANDS SURRENDER

EVEN before the formal surrender of the Japanese government, the enemy commanders of Marcus Island and of Mille atoll in the Marshall Islands had capitulated to American forces. The largest scale island surrender came shortly after the beginning of the occupation of the main Japanese Islands. The commander of the 31st Japanese Army committed the islands of Truk, Wake, the Palaus, Mortlock, Mille, Ponape, Kusaie, Jaluit, Maleolap, Wotje, Enderby, Mereyon, Rota, and Pagan to the United States. On Truk alone the surrender involved 130,000 Japanese military personnel.

While the naval and air forces of Japan were either destroyed or rendered impotent by our sea-air blockade, her army was still more than 4 million strong and better trained, and larger than at the time of the initial attack at Pearl Harbor.

Never before in the history of warfare has there been a more convincing example of the effectiveness of sea power than when, despite this undefeated, well armed, and highly efficient army, Japan surrendered her homeland unconditionally to the enemy without even a token resistance.

The devastation wrought by past bombings plus the destruction of the atomic bombs spelled nothing less than extinction for Japan. The bases from which these attacks were launched—Saipan, Iwo Jima, and Okinawa—were to have been the spring boards for the mightiest sea-borne invasion yet conceived by man. The "fighting fleets" of the United States which had made possible every invasion victory for America and her allies were ready and waiting. The Japanese had two alternatives; to fight and face destruction, or to surrender. The Imperial Japanese Empire chose to surrender.

W.F. Halsey

Fleet Adm. Chester W. Nimitz of the United States signs the Japanese surrender document aboard the U.S.S. *Missouri* in Tokyo Bay, September 2, 1945. Standing immediately behind Nimitz, from left to right, are General of the Army Douglas MacArthur, Adm. William Halsey, and Rear Adm. Frederick Sherman. (Navy Department photograph.)

A 'KID' AT 17 GOES TO WAR   1943

1943

WENDELL ANDERSON enlisted in the United States Navy (September). Later (after 'boots') he was assigned to the 33'd Special Seabee Battalion. Boarded HMS (His majesty's ship of NORWAY) in the fall of '43) HMS TORENS. The ship was nothing but a 'tramp steamer' our navy procured the vessel by confiscation because the Ship was considered enemy as it plied the oceans under the Axis flag...Hitler's Navy! ...After months of training we were loaded and headed out of Oxnard California...due South. We crossed the Equator somewhere near the Christmas Islands, and then 'hard-right' due-west and making our first stop off the island of GUADALCANAL. A few days later we continued our 'sailing' West to the Southern most tip of NEW GUINEA, Melanie Bay. We moved up to HOLLANDIA, NEW GUINEA where we sat for a month (on the equator) waiting for incoming ships to join us in 'convoy' for the invasion of the PHILIPPINES. All in fall of ....

1944

My outfit learned QUICK! ... we were under attack by Japanese aircraft daily as our Convoy drew closer to our destination LEYTE, PHILIPPINES. Many of the ships of our 'Convoy' were hit, on fire or sinking, and had fallen out of 'Convoy'.

I thank GOD and Admiral Halsey for his masterful maneuvers to defeat JAPANESE war ships in an around the 'pass' between LEYTE and SAMAR, CEBU, PHILIPPINES. Halsey and his 7th fleet of Warships took out a number of Japanese ships that had their 'AIM' at destroying our troop transports and supply ships that arrived safely into LEYTE harbor early November of 1944.

ORAL HISTORY PROJECT TAPS VETERANS' EXPERIENCES

Incredible stories, now shared

WAR MEMORIES: Archive ensures voices won't be lost to the future

By BILLY COX
billy.cox@heraldtribune.com

SARASOTA — "How do you teach a kid about killing? They don't know the horrors of this stuff," says Wendell Anderson. "All they've got are the fictionalized formats on television."

For the 86-year-old World War II veteran, the question of what to share and what to withhold is not an academic exercise. Even now, memories of sudden death in the Pacific Theater dictate his behavior on Veterans Day.

"I can't even go to the parades anymore," he says. "To me, Nov. 11 is just a funeral dirge."

And yet, several years ago, the former Navy Seabee agreed to sit before a camera and compress his war experience into a 21-minute video.

The Sarasota resident skipped the more lurid aspects — what they lifted from the bodies of the enemy, a Filipino woman pounding a gold tooth from the mouth of a Japanese corpse — and settled on more sanitized but no less illuminating imagery: bouts with dengue and typhoid fevers, for instance.

Anderson, who was with the U.S. invasion force as it rolled into the Philippines in 1944, shared his story with Venice resident Ted Koszarski, who began taping veterans' tales in

Wendell Anderson, a former Navy Seabee, shares a 1945 photograph of himself, center, in the Philippines. His is among many veterans' stories featured in a local archive.
TOP: COURTESY PHOTO; ABOVE: E. SKYLAR LITHERLAND

FOR MORE INFORMATION

■ To read more stories about area veterans, go to www .heraldtribune.com/veterans.

■ To learn more about Ted Koszarski's oral history project, go to www.veterans memorialarchive.com.

■ For more information about Riverview High School's veterans project, call 923-1484.

■ Additional information about the Library of Congress' Veterans History Project can be found online at www.loc.gov/vets/.

MORE STORIES INSIDE

■ While most government offices are closed for Veterans Day, some schools will remain open and use the time to teach students about war, history and people who sacrifice.1B

■ At long last, Vietnam vets get a 'welcome home.' 7A

See VETERANS on 7A

Veterans share stories with new generations

Wendell Anderson, at top left, was a Navy Seabee.
STAFF PHOTO / E. SKYLAR LITHERLAND

VETERANS *from 1A*

1995 when he was with a public access television station in New York.

Today, Koszarski's oral-history library has 637 entries, mostly from World War II, and he has posted many on his Veterans Memorial Archive Web page. A year ago, he began contemplating their value to a new generation.

"Two things make great TV: production value and intimacy," says Koszarski, "and that's what these incredible stories have going for them. I think the possibilities for the classroom are unlimited. I think it could inspire poetry, or letters; you could create artwork or music from the themes they raise."

Among the first people he approached was state Sen. Nancy Detert, who saw immediate potential.

"One of my grandsons, Ryan, was so impressed when a real live actual World War II veteran spoke to his class in the second grade," recalls Detert. "He started looking into it and asked, 'Do we have any World War II veterans in our family?' and I told him his great-grandfather, my husband's dad, was a pilot in World War II.

"I thought Ted was really on to something, but he was talking about starting at the state level. I said, 'Why not start locally first?'"

Koszarski followed Detert's leads into the Sarasota County school system. The idea took root at Riverview High, where media specialist Myra Plescia is using Veterans Day as the kickoff to build Riverview's own archives.

"We're really excited because we've got some talented students and lots of veterans in this area," Plescia says. "We want to get the word out and invite them to share their stories with us."

Plescia is basing her model on the Library of Congress' Veterans History Project in Washington, which suggests 30 minutes as an ideal length.

"The key is to come to the interview prepared," Plescia says. "That means the students are really going to

World War II veteran Wendell Anderson was with the U.S. invasion force in the Philippines. COURTESY PHOTO

have to do their homework."

Established by Congress in 2000, the Veterans History Project has collected 70,000 veterans' interviews over the past decade, 10 percent which are now available online. Project coordinator Jessica Souva says it sent related material to every high school in America during the buildup to Ken Burns' 2007 PBS documentary "The War," and that Florida's large number of military retirees make this one of its target states.

Souva says the University of Florida, Florida State University and the University of Central Florida have recently embarked upon organizing oral-history collections. "What we would really like is for everyone who logs onto our site on Veterans Day to pledge to interview a veteran," she says. "We'd like to get 10,000 new stories."

Interestingly, among the last World War I veteran interviews in the Veterans History Project archives is the late Ernest Pusey of Bradenton. Pusey, a Navy veteran, died in 2006 at age 111. The Library of Congress' database posted transcripts of an audio inter-

view conducted by friends, but Koszarski managed to shoot video of Pusey in 2005, which he hopes to upload to his Web site soon.

Only one American survivor of World War I — the conflict that inspired Veterans Day — remains alive. Frank Buckles, 109, lives in Charles Town, West Virginia.

"So many of the guys I've got on file have passed on," Koszarski says. "I've had a lot of people tell me about how they've played some of these interviews at memorial services, and how much it meant. You don't need any special skills to do this. You just need to be really interested."

Although oral histories may enlighten future generations to the personal realities of specific conflicts, the man who saw the American fleet mangled by bombs, torpedoes and kamikazes doubts their ability to steer humanity from repeating its mistakes.

"Ted's onto a project the significance of which I don't even think he understands," Anderson says. "Hopefully his work will still be around long after all of us are gone."

Seabees played critical war role

The Navy Seabees, short for construction battalion, played a critical role in World War II by building the roadways, air strips, bridges and basic infrastructure that supported the Allied victory.

After going operational in 1942, some 325,000 Seabees operated on six continents during the war. Sarasota's Wendell Anderson followed the 33rd Special Seabee Battalion into New Guinea and The Philippines, where it began erecting air bases on the island of Samar.

"The conditions were pretty horrible," recalls Anderson of his trek through the Pacific. "I saw more guys die from disease than anything else. It was pretty rough stuff."

The Seabees have participated in American military and peacekeeping missions ever since. Whether helping South Florida claw out of Hurricane Andrew's rubble in 1992 or providing construction relief earlier this year to an earthquake-shattered Haiti, the outfit is renowned for its flexibility.

Afghanistan is among the Seabees' most recent deployments, where units are building bases, improving roads and drilling water wells for the local population.

— *Billy Cox*

YESTERDAY — PHILIPPINES 1944 — TODAY 2010 FLORIDA

'D' DAY + 2
OUR FOX HOLE!
... STRANGE, YOU DIG
DEEPER EVERY NITE!

FIRST ITEM : WATER

"LOOKS" IS IT FRESH WATER
OR ?

---AND IT BECAME THE
33 RD BATTALIONS 'WATER
DEPT'

Surrender in the Philippine Islands

**Camp John Hay, Baguio, Luzon,
Philippine Islands,
September 3, 1945.**

In compliance with the Instrument of Surrender, the general capitulation at Tokyo Bay was followed by the surrender of individual Japanese armies in the fields of combat in the Far East.

The honor of receiving the surrender of the Japanese in the Philippines was given to the distinguished figure who had stood beside General MacArthur at the Tokyo Bay ceremony—Lt. Gen. Jonathan M. Wainwright, who had fought gallantly and suffered defeat and captivity in the Philippines. The ceremony took place on September 3, 1945. The setting offered a contrast to that of Tokyo Bay. It was Camp John Hay at Baguio, in Mountain Province on Luzon in the Philippines.

For Japan, the "Instrument of Surrender of the Japanese and Japanese-Controlled Armed Forces in the Philippine Islands" was signed at 10 minutes after noon, local time, by Gen. Tomoyuki Yamashita, Imperial Japanese Army Highest Commander, Imperial Japanese Army in the Philippines; and Vice Adm. Denhici Okochi, Imperial Japanese Navy Highest Commander, Imperial Japanese Navy in the Philippines.

Wendell

From: <CaptainJH@aol.com>
To: <wendellanderson@comcast.net>
Sent: Saturday, September 23, 2006 8:23 PM
Subject: Invasion of Japan

This is a really good read... Bob is an old friend of mine, a retired doctor and an ex P-38 pilot... Marc "Brig Gen R. Clements USAF ret"

Deep in the recesses of the National Archives in Washington, D.C., hidden for nearly four decades lie thousands of pages of yellowing and dusty documents stamped "Top Secret". These documents, now declassified, are the plans for Operation Downfall, the invasion of Japan during World War II. Only a few Americans in 1945 were aware of the elaborate plans that had been prepared for the Allied Invasion of the Japanese home islands. Even fewer today are aware of the defenses the Japanese had prepared to counter the invasion had it been launched. Operation Downfall was finalized during the spring and summer of 1945. It called for two massive military undertakings to be carried out in succession and aimed at the heart of the Japanese Empire.

In the first invasion - code named "Operation Olympic"- American combat troops would land on Japan by amphibious assault during the early morning hours of November 1, 1945 - 61 years ago. Fourteen combat divisions of soldiers and Marines would land on heavily fortified and defended Kyushu, the southernmost of the Japanese home islands, after an unprecedented naval and aerial bombardment.

The second invasion on March 1, 1946 - code named "Operation Coronet"- would send at least 22 divisions against 1 million Japanese defenders on the main island of Honshu and the Tokyo Plain. Its goal: the unconditional surrender of Japan.

With the exception of a part of the British Pacific Fleet, Operation Downfall was to be a strictly American operation. It called for using the entire Marine Corps, the entire Pacific Navy, elements of the 7th Army Air Force, the 8 Air Force (recently redeployed from Europe), 10th Air Force and the American Far Eastern Air Force. More than 1.5 million combat soldiers, with 3 million more in support or more than 40% of all servicemen still in uniform in 1945 - would be directly involved in the two amphibious assaults.Casuatties were expected to be extremely heavy.

Admiral William Leahy estimated that there would be more than 250,000 Americans killed or wounded on Kyushu alone. General Charles Willoughby, chief of intelligence for General Douglas MacArthur, the Supreme Commander of the Southwest Pacific, estimated American casualties would be one million men by the fall of 1946. Willoughby's own intelligence staff considered this to be a conservative estimate.

During the summer of 1945, America had little time to prepare for such an endeavor, but top military leaders were in almost unanimous agreement that an invasion was necessary.

While naval blockade and strategic bombing of Japan was considered to be useful, General

MacArthur, for instance, did not believe a blockade would bring about an unconditional surrender. The advocates for invasion agreed that while a naval blockade chokes, it does not kill; and though strategic bombing might destroy cities, it leaves whole armies intact.

So on May 25, 1945, the Joint Chiefs of Staff, after extensive deliberation, issued to General MacArthur, Admiral Chester Nimitz, and Army Air Force General Henry Arnold, the top secret directive to proceed with the invasion of Kyushu. The target date was after the typhoon season.

President Truman approved the plans for the invasions July 24. Two days later, the United Nations issued the Potsdam Proclamation, which called upon Japan to surrender unconditionally or face total destruction. Three days later, the Japanese governmental news agency broadcast to the world that Japan would ignore the proclamation and would refuse to surrender. During this sane period it was learned — via monitoring Japanese radio broadcasts that Japan had closed all schools and mobilized its school children, was arming its civilian population and was fortifying caves and building underground defenses.

Operation Olympic called for a four pronged assault on Kyushu. Its purpose was to seize and control the southern one-third of that island and establish naval and air bases, to tighten the naval blockade of the home islands, to destroy units of the main Japanese army and to support the later invasion of the Tokyo Plain.

The preliminary invasion would began October 27 when the 40th Infantry Division would land on a series of small islands west and southwest of Kyushu. At the same time, the 158th Regimental Combat Team would invade and occupy a small island 28 miles south of Kyushu. On these islands, seaplane bases would be established and radar would be set up to provide advance air warning for the invasion fleet, to serve as fighter direction centers for the carrier-based aircraft and to provide an emergency anchorage for the invasion fleet, should things not go well on the day of the invasion. As the invasion grew imminent, the massive firepower of the Navy - the Third and Fifth Fleets -- would approach Japan. The Third Fleet, under Admiral William "Bull" Halsey, with its big guns and naval aircraft, would provide strategic support for the operation against Honshu and Hokkaido. Halsey's fleet would be composed of battleships, heavy cruisers, destroyers, dozens of support ships and three fast carrier task groups. From these carriers, hundreds of Navy fighters, dive bombers and torpedo planes would hit targets all over the island of Honshu. The 3,000 ship Fifth Fleet, under Admiral Raymond Spruance, would carry the invasion troops. Several days before the invasion, the battleships, heavy cruisers and destroyers would pour thousands of tons of high explosives into the target areas. They would not cease the bombardment until after the land forces had been launched. During the early morning hours of November 1, the invasion would begin. Thousands of soldiers and Marines would pour ashore on beaches all along the eastern, southeastern, southern and western coasts of Kyushu. Waves of Helldivers, Dauntless dive bombers, Avengers, Corsairs, and Hellcats from 66 aircraft carriers would bomb, rocket and strafe enemy defenses, gun emplacements and troop concentrations along the beaches.

The Eastern Assault Force consisting of the 25th, 33rd, and 41st Infantry Divisions, would land near Miyaski, at beaches called Austin, Buick, Cadillac, Chevrolet, Chrysler, and Ford, and move inland to attempt to capture the city and its nearby airfield. The Southern Assault Force, consisting of the 1st Cavalry Division, the 43rd Division and America! Division would land inside Ariake Bay at beaches labeled DeSoto, Dusenberg, Essex, Ford, and Franklin and attempt to capture Shibushi and the city of Kanoya and its airfield.

On the western shore of Kyushu, at beaches Pontiac, Reo, Rolls Royce, Saxon, Star, Studebaker, Stutz, Winston and Zephyr, the V Amphibious Corps would land the 2nd, 3rd, and 5th Marine Divisions, sending half of its force inland to Sendai and the other half to the port city of Kagoshima.

On November 4, the Reserve Force, consisting of the 81st and 98th Infantry Divisions and the 11th Airborne Division, after feigning an attack on the island of Shikoku, would be landed — if not needed elsewhere — near Kaimondake, near the southernmost tip of Kagoshima Bay, at the beaches designated Locomobile, Lincoln, LaSalle, Hupmobile, Moon, Mercedes, Maxwell, Overland, Oldsmobile, Packard, and Plymouth.

Olympic was not just a plan for invasion, but for conquest and occupation as well. It was expected to take four months to achieve its objective, with the three fresh American divisions per month to be landed in support of that operation if needed. If all went well with Olympic, Coronet would be launched March 1,1946. Coronet would be twice the size of Olympic, with as many as 28 divisions landing on Honshu.

All along the coast east of Tokyo, the American 1st Army would land the 5th, 7th, 27th, 44th, 86th, and 96th Infantry Divisions, along with the 4th and 6th Marine Divisions.

At Sagami Bay, just south of Tokyo, the entire 8th and 10th Armies would strike north and east to clear the long western shore of Tokyo Bay and attempt to go as far as Yokohama. The assault troops landing south of Tokyo would be the 4th, 6th, 8th, 24th, 31st, 37th, 38th, and 8th Infantry Divisions, along with the 13th and 20th Armored Divisions.

Following the initial assault, eight more divisions - the 2nd, 28th, 35th, 91st, 95th, 97th, and 104th Infantry Divisions and the 11th Airborne Division — would be landed. if additional troops were needed, as expected, other divisions redeployed from Europe and undergoing training in the United States would be shipped to Japan in what was hoped to be the final push.

Captured Japanese documents and post war interrogations of Japanese military leaders disclose that information concerning the number of Japanese planes available for the defense of the home islands was dangerously in error.

During the sea battle at Okinawa alone, Japanese Kamikaze aircraft sank 32 Allied ships and damaged more than 400 others. But during the summer of 1945, American top brass concluded that the Japanese had spent their air force since American bombers and fighters daily flew unmolested over Japan.

What the military leaders did not know was that by the end of July the Japanese had been saving all aircraft, fuel, and pilots in reserve, and had been feverishly building new planes for the decisive battle for their homeland.

As part of Ketsu-Go, the name for the plan to defend Japan — the Japanese were building 20 suicide takeoff strips in southern Kyushu with underground hangars. They also had 35 camouflaged airfields and nine seaplane bases.

On the night before the expected invasion, 50 Japanese seaplane bombers, 100 former carrier aircraft and 50 land based army planes were to be launched in a suicide attack on the fleet. The Japanese had 58 more airfields in Korea, western Honshu and Shikoku, which also were to be used for massive suicide attacks.

Allied intelligence had established that the Japanese had no more than 2,500 aircraft of which they guessed 300 would be deployed in suicide attacks. In August 1945, however, unknown to Allied intelligence, the Japanese still had 5,651 army and 7,074 navy aircraft, for a total of 12,725 planes of all types. Every village had some type of aircraft manufacturing activity. Hidden in mines, railway tunnels, under viaducts and in basements of department stores, work was being done to construct new planes.

Additionally, the Japanese were building newer and more effective models of the Okka, a rocket-propelled bomb much like the German V-1, but flown by a suicide pilot. When the invasion became imminent, Ketsu-Go called for a fourfold aerial plan of attack to destroy up to 800 Allied ships.

While Allied ships were approaching Japan, but still in the open seas, an initial force of 2,000 army and navy fighters were to fight to the death to control the skies over Kyushu. A second force of 330 navy combat pilots were to attack the main body of the task force to keep it from using its fire support and air cover to protect the troop carrying transports. While these two forces were engaged, a third force of 825 suicide planes was to hit the American transports.

As the invasion convoys approached their anchorages, another 2,000 suicide planes were to be launched in waves of 200 to 300, to be used in hour by hour attacks. By mid-morning of the first day of the invasion, most of the American land-based aircraft would be forced to return to their bases, leaving the defense against the suicide planes to the carrier pilots and the shipboard gunners.

Carrier pilots crippled by fatigue would have to land time and time again to rearm and refuel. Guns would malfunction from the heat of continuous firing and ammunition would become scarce. Gun crews would be exhausted by nightfall, but still the waves of kamikaze would continue. With the fleet hovering off the beaches, all remaining Japanese aircraft would be committed to nonstop suicide attacks, which the Japanese hoped could be sustained for 10 days. The Japanese planned to coordinate their air strikes with attacks from the 40 remaining submarines from the Imperial Navy — some armed with Long Lance torpedoes with a range of 20 miles — when the invasion fleet was 180 miles off Kyushu.

The Imperial Navy had 23 destroyers and two cruisers which were operational. These ships were to be used to counterattack the American invasion. A number of the destroyers were to be beached at the last minute to be used as anti-invasion gun platforms.

Once offshore, the invasion fleet would be forced to defend not only against the attacks from the

air, but would also be confronted with suicide attacks from sea. Japan had established a suicide naval attack unit of midget submarines, human torpedoes and exploding motorboats.

The goal of the Japanese was to shatter the invasion before the landing. The Japanese were convinced the Americans would back off or become so demoralized that they would then accept a less-than-unconditional surrender and a more honorable and face-saving end for the Japanese.

But as horrible as the battle of Japan would be off the beaches, it would be on Japanese soil that the American forces would face the most rugged and fanatical defense encountered during the war.

Throughout the island-hopping Pacific campaign, Allied troops had always out numbered the Japanese by 2 to 1 and sometimes 3 to 1. In Japan it would be different. By virtue of a combination of cunning, guesswork, and brilliant military reasoning, a number of Japan's top military leaders were able to deduce, not only when, but where, the United States would land its first invasion forces.

Facing the 14 American divisions landing at Kyushu would be 14 Japanese divisions, 7 independent mixed brigades, 3 tank brigades and thousands of naval troops. On Kyushu the odds would be 3 to 2 in favor of the Japanese, with 790,000 enemy defenders against 550,000 Americans. This time the bulk of the Japanese defenders would not be the poorly trained and ill-equipped labor battalions that the Americans had faced in the earlier campaigns.

The Japanese defenders would be the hard core of the home army. These troops were well-fed and well equipped. They were familiar with the terrain, had stockpiles of arms and ammunition, and had developed an effective system of transportation and supply almost invisible from the air. Many of these Japanese troops were the elite of the army, and they were swollen with a fanatical fighting spirit.

Japan's network of beach defenses consisted of offshore mines, thousands of suicide scuba divers attacking landing craft, and mines planted on the beaches. Coming ashore, the American Eastern amphibious assault forces at Miyazaki would face three Japanese divisions, and two others poised for counterattack. Awaiting the Southeastern attack force at Ariake Bay was an entire division and at least one mixed infantry brigade.

On the western shores of Kyushu, the Marines would face the most brutal opposition. Along the invasion beaches would be the three Japanese divisions, a tank brigade, a mixed infantry brigade and an artillery command. Components of two divisions would also be poised to launch counterattacks.

If not needed to reinforce the primary landing beaches, the American Reserve Force would be landed at the base of Kagoshima Bay November 4, where they would be confronted by two mixed infantry brigades, parts of two infantry divisions and thousands of naval troops.

All along the invasion beaches, American troops would face coastal batteries, anti-landing obstacles and a network of heavily fortified pillboxes, bunkers, and underground fortresses. As

Americans waded ashore, they would face intense artillery and mortar fire as they worked their way through concrete rubble and barbed-wire entanglements arranged to funnel them into the muzzles of these Japanese guns.

On the beaches and beyond would be hundreds of Japanese machine gun positions, beach mines, booby traps, trip-wire mines and sniper units. Suicide units concealed in "spider holes" would engage the troops as they passed nearby. In the heat of battle, Japanese infiltration units would be sent to reap havoc in the American lines by cutting phone and communication lines. Some of the Japanese troops would be in American uniform, English-speaking Japanese officers were assigned to break in on American radio traffic to call off artillery fire, to order retreats and to further confuse troops. Other infiltration with demolition charges strapped on their chests or backs would attempt to blow up American tanks, artillery pieces and ammunition stores as they were unloaded ashore.

Beyond the beaches were large artillery pieces situated to bring down a curtain of fire on the beach. Some of these large guns were mounted on railroad tracks running in and out of caves protected by concrete and steel.

The battle for Japan would be won by what Simon Bolivar Buckner, a lieutenant general in the Confederate army during the Civil War, had called "Prairie Dog Warfare." This type of fighting was almost unknown to the ground troops in Europe and the Mediterranean. It was peculiar only to the soldiers and Marines who fought the Japanese on islands all over the Pacific — at Tarawa, Saipan, Iwo Jima and Okinawa.

Prairie Dog Warfare was a battle for yards, feet and sometimes inches. It was brutal, deadly and dangerous form of combat aimed at an underground, heavily fortified, non-retreating enemy.

In the mountains behind the Japanese beaches were underground networks of caves, bunkers, command posts and hospitals connected by miles of tunnels with dozens of entrances and exits. Some of these complexes could hold up to 1,000 troops.

In addition to the use of poison gas and bacteriological warfare (which the Japanese had experimented with), Japan mobilized its citizenry.

Had Olympic come about, the Japanese civilian population, inflamed by a national slogan - "One Hundred Million Will Die for the Emperor and Nation" - were prepared to fight to the death. Twenty Eight Million Japanese had become a part of the National Volunteer Combat Force. They were armed with ancient rifles, lunge mines, satchel charges, Molotov cocktails and one-shot black powder mortars. Others were armed with swords, long bows, axes and bamboo spears. The civilian units were to be used in nighttime attacks, hit and run maneuvers, delaying actions and massive suicide charges at the weaker American positions.

At the early stage of the invasion, 1,000 Japanese and American soldiers would be dying every hour. The invasion of Japan never became a reality because on August 6, 1945, an atomic bomb was exploded over Hiroshima. Three days later, a second bomb was dropped on Nagasaki. Within days the war with Japan was at a close.

Had these bombs not been dropped and had the invasion been launched as scheduled, combat casualties in Japan would have been at a minimum of the tens of thousands. Every foot of Japanese soil would have been paid for by Japanese and American lives.

One can only guess at how many civilians would have committed suicide in their homes or in futile mass military attacks. In retrospect, the 1 million American men who were to be the casualties of the invasion, were instead lucky enough to survive the war.

Intelligence studies and military estimates made 50 years ago, and not latter-day speculation, dearly indicate that the battle for Japan might well have resulted in the biggest blood-bath in the history of modern warfare.

Far worse would be what might have happened to Japan as a nation and as a culture. When the invasion came, it would have come after several months of fire bombing all of the remaining Japanese cities. The cost in human life that resulted from the two atomic blasts would be small in comparison to the total number of Japanese lives that would have been lost by this aerial devastation.

With American forces locked in combat in the south of Japan, little could have prevented the Soviet Union from marching into the northern half of the Japanese home islands. Japan today cold be divided much like Korea and Germany.

The world was spared the cost of Operation Downfall, however, because Japan formally surrendered to the United Nations September 2, 1945, and World War II was over.

The aircraft carriers, cruisers and transport ships scheduled to carry the invasion troops to .Japan, ferried home American troops in a gigantic operation called Magic Carpet.

In the fall of 1945, in the aftermath of the war, few people concerned themselves with the invasion plans. Following the surrender, the classified documents, maps, diagrams and appendices for Operation Downfall were packed away in boxes and eventually stored at the National Archives. These plans that called for the invasion of Japan paint a vivid description of what might have been one of the most horrible campaigns in the history of man.

The fact that the story of the invasion of Japan is locked up in the National Archives and is not told in our history books is something for which all Americans can be thankful.

I had the distinct privilege of being assigned as later commander of the 8090th PACUSA detach, 20th AAF, and one of the personal pilots of then Brig General Fred Irving USMA 17 when he was commanding general of Western Pacific Base Command. We had a brand new C-46F tail number 8546. It was different from the rest of the C-46 line in that it was equipped with Hamilton Hydromatic props whereas the others had Curtis electrics. On one of the many flights we had 14 Generals and Admirals aboard on an inspection trip to Saipan and Tinian. Notable aboard was General Thomas C. Handy, who had signed the operational order to drop the atomic bombs Dn Japan. President Truman's orders were verbal . He never signed an order to drop the bombs

http://www.nucleaitles.org/menu/library/correspondence/handy-thomas/cob_ handy_1945-07-25.htm

On this particular flight, about half way from Guam to Tinian, a full Colonel(General Handy's aide) came up forward and told me that General Handy would like to come up and look around. I told him, "Hell yes, he can fly the airplane if he wants to, sir <BG>"

He came up and sat in the copilots seat, put on the headset and we started chatting. I asked him if he ever regretted dropping the bombs. His answer was, "Certainly not. We saved a million lives on both sides by doing it. It was the right thing to do"

I never forgot that trip and the honor of being able to talk to General Handy. I was a Lt at the time.

A postscript about General Irving. He was one of the finest gentleman I ever met. He was the oldest living graduate of West Point when he passed on at 100+.

He was on of three Generals who had the honor of being both the "Supe" and "Corn" of West Point. I think the other gentleman were BG Sladen class of 1890 and BG Stewart Class of 1896 I am very happy the invasion never came off because if it had I don't think I would be writing this today. We were to provide air support for the boots on the ground guys. The small arms fire would have been devastating and lethal as hell to fly through.. Just think what it would have been like on the ground

But, C'est la vive. You do what needs to be done. You don't act like gutless

"There Would Be NO United States of America"

"If It Weren't For The United States Military"

Bob

JAPAN SURRENDERS 1945

Surrender Documents

The document that the Japanese representatives were to sign was the official Instrument of Surrender, prepared by the War Department in Washington, D. C., and approved by President Truman. It sets out in eight short paragraphs the complete capitulation of Japan. The opening words: "We, acting by command of and in behalf of the Emperor of Japan" signify the importance attached to the role of the Emperor by the Americans who drafted the document. The short second paragraph goes straight to the heart of the matter: "We hereby proclaim the unconditional surrender to the Allied Powers of the Japanese Imperial General Headquarters and of all Japanese armed forces and all armed forces under Japanese control wherever situated."

That morning, on the deck of the battleship in Tokyo Bay, the Japanese envoys stood before General MacArthur and the other Allied representatives and wrote their names on the marked lines on the Instrument of Surrender. The time was recorded as four minutes past nine o'clock:

After Shigemitsu and Umezu had affixed their signatures to the Instrument of Surrender, Gen. Douglas MacArthur, Commander in the Southwest Pacific and Supreme Commander for the Allied Powers, also signed. He accepted the Japanese surrender "for the United States, Republic of China, United Kingdom, and the Union of Soviet Socialist Republics, and in the interests of the other United Nations at war with Japan."

The Allied representatives who then signed the documents were all distinguished

military men. Adm.Chester W. Nimitz who, as Commander in the Central Pacific, had headed the largest fighting fleet in history, signed as the U.S. representative. Gen. Hsu Yung-Chiang signed for the Republic of China, Adm. Sir Bruce A. Fraser for the United Kingdom, Lt. Gen. Kuzma Derevyanko for the Soviet Union, Gen. Sir Thomas Blarney for the Commonwealth of Australia, Col. L. Moore Cosgrave for Canada, Gen. Jacques Le Clerc for France, Adm. C. E. L. Helfrich for the Netherlands, and Air Vice Marshal Leonard M. 1st for New Zealand.

At General MacArthur's side as he signed were two distinguished Allied soldiers who had been prisoners of war of the Japanese: Lt. Gen. Jonathan M. Wainwright, captured after his surrender at Corregidor in 1942, and Lt. Gen. Arthur E. Percival, British Commander at the time of the fall of the Singapore garrison, also in 1942.

Following the surrender ceremonies, Col. Bernard Thielen brought the surrender document and a second Imperial rescript back to Washington, D. C., arriving shortly after 9 P.M. on September 6. The next morning, Friday, the documents were presented by Th ie len to President Truman in a formal White House ceremony. At 11 A.M., Wednesday, September 12, following a dignified ceremony led by General Wainwright, the documents were exhibited at the National Archives of the United States. Finally, on October 1, 1945, they were formally accessioned by the National Archives.

In order to facilitate the surrender of Japanese forces in all parts of the Pacific and the mainland of Asia, Emperor Hirohito issued his second rescript, also on September 2. This document had been dictated to the Japanese emissaries by General MacArthur in Manila. The second rescript called upon all Japanese military personnel to comply with the terms of the general Instrument of Surrender. In order that the full significance of the surrender might be emphasized and a prolonged guerilla conflict averted, the rescript was countersigned by Prime Minister Higashikun i and contained the names of the entire Japanese Cabinet, emphasizing their submission to the Supreme Commander for the Allied Powers.

The signatures included those of such prominent politicians as Fumimaro Konoe, a member of the Imperial Family and a former Prime Minister; Mitsumasa Yonai, Navy minister in three previous Cabinets and Commander in Chief of the Joint Staff; and Sadamu Shimomura, former Minister of War.

Some Pixs' About 'our'

VIEW OF OUR MAIN STREET !

'OUR' HOSPITAL ON SITE

MY TENT HOME OF TWO + YEARS

IN DRESS UNIFORM EVERY DAY !

CALLED A 'RECON'

OUT FOR A SUNDAY DRIVE

33ᴿᴰ CAMP SITE ___

FROM A PATH IN THE JUNGLE WE BUILT OUR OWN 'SUPER' HIGHWAY

THIS IS A 'MULE TEAM

WE BUILT OUR OWN THEATRE AWAITED THE USO GIRLS - HUH?

--- OUR MOTOR POOL OR GAS STATION

__ANOTHER VIEW OF HOME ON SAMAR

"PEACE BE WITH YOU"

S miles returned to the faces of the folks of SAMAR, PHILIPPINES. The kids quickly returned to their fun of their LEYTE GULF, their bay waters were theirs to play! THE WAR WAS OVER...

The 'PESO money printed by the Japanese was discontinued as the monitory medium of exchange. The return of the PHILIPPINE PESO was re-introduced, and welcomed.

The PHILIPPINE people, I learned, were very Entrepreneurial and moved quickly into their trading and manufacturing their wares and products.

I remained six months after the war was over. I saw many interesting happenings relative to the 'spoils of war' (military product and equipment disappeared). One day, someone asked of me, "what happened to all those 'junked' airplanes?" He appeared in officer's uniform. I reminded him that our Congressional 'tour' came to SAMAR for basic inspection! Many months previous my buddies told me of covering the aircraft with sand a mountain high.

Well, a couple of days later the bull-dozers were uncovering those planes. The 'junk' aircraft were being loaded aboard a French ship!

NuF CED

▲ *Ships of the US fleet assembled off Luzon. Landing craft heading for shore can be seen in the bottom of the photograph.*

JANUARY 1

LAND WAR, *CAROLINE ISLANDS*

US Army forces are landed on Fais Island in the Carolines with the objective of capturing and destroying a Japanese radio station.

JANUARY 2–8

LAND WAR, *PHILIPPINES*

The US high command in the Philippines re-deploys the Sixth Army under General Krueger from Leyte to positions off Lingayen Gulf on Luzon.

AERIAL KAMIKAZE ATTACKS

On October 19, 1944, Vice-Admiral Onishi Takijino ordered the formation of a kamikaze force to intercept Allied shipping around the Philippines, officially termed Tokubetsu Koge-ki Tai (Special Attack Group). The term kamikaze literally means "divine wind", referring to the typhoons that destroyed Kublai Khan's fleets in 1274 and 1281, saving Japan from a Mongol invasion. Kamikaze pilots were all volunteers, usually very young, who were given the most rudimentary flying training and piloted old or battle-repaired aircraft, usually with only enough fuel to reach their attack destination. Fed on a

A group of kamikaze pilots are given a ceremonial cup of sake prior to their one-way mission.

Bushido ideology of death being preferable to defeat, they accepted that to return from a kamikaze mission invited disgrace.

The kamikaze pilots inflicted a horrifying experience on the sailors and soldiers of the US Pacific Fleet. Although hundreds of suicide aircraft were shot down before reaching their targets (the pilots did not have experience of air combat, and could not fly low beneath US radar), thousands still got through. The first mass attack of 55 kamikaze aircraft came on October 23–26, 1944, around Leyte, sinking five ships (including the carrier USS *St Lo*) and damaging 40 others, 23 severely. In April 1945, the kamikaze attacks reached a frenzied pitch off Okinawa. Around 1900 suicide aircraft attacked in "kikusui" (floating chrysanthemum) waves of up to 320 planes at a time. Thirty-six US ships were sunk, and three hundred and sixty-eight damaged. In total, Japan lost 5000 pilots in suicide actions during the war.

1945

The last year of the Pacific war saw heavy fighting on all fronts. Though US war production far outstripped that of Japan, overwhelming superiority in ships, aircraft and tanks did not translate into easy victories. On Iwo Jima and Okinawa US forces suffered heavy losses, which boded ill for the invasion of Japan itself. The Americans thus dropped atomic bombs on Japan to hasten the end of the war.

▼ *A kamikaze aircraft dives towards the light cruiser USS* Columbia *during the Lingayen Gulf invasion on January 6, 1945. The ship was hit by two kamikaze aircraft and severely damaged.*

Kamikaze attacks intensify around Leyte Gulf. Today, the destroyer USS Abner Road is sunk and the destroyers USS Anderson, USS Claxton and USS Ammen are badly damaged by suicide attacks. Dive-bombers damage two other destroyers. AIR WAR, LEYTE GULF

USS Indianapolis CA-35

CRUISER INDIANAPOLIS SUNK
BY JAPANESE U-BOAT—JULY 30, 1945

...A TRAGIC LOSS OF LIFE on that night, just 13 days til the end of the War with Japan!

A Japanese submarine came up for air in the Philippine Sea, about 50-80 miles off SAMAR and the Leyte Gulf. The untimely event was a FULL moon that night. Imagine an ideal Submarine setting alone on a 'black' ocean, and across its' bow appears an outline of a like-new' Cruiser, and just an outline or silhouette of a major Fighting Ship! A 'by-chance' trophy of war! The Captain must have called for 'emergency... battle ready dive'. He fired 2 torpedoes that pierced the broad-side of the 'darkened ship' sinking the INDIANAPOLIS within 29 minutes! The 'Indy' had nearly 1100 men on board; ...the torpedoes scored!

The injured and dead claimed 780. 320 men survived. Of all our Naval ships engaged in WWII the sinking of the INDIANAPOLIS was one of 3 most disastrous happenings to our Naval Ships of the war.

Around midnight that night I was on my usual night shift of duty...a couple of Seabees and myself were standing outside the Mess Hall 'chatting'. Our subject was; "The war is ending and we were talking about going home!"

Together, we saw this 'FLASH' in the Northeast sky! "WHAT THE HELL WAS THAT?" one of the fellows said. "SOME POOR BASTARD GOT HIT!" End of the 'strange light' question.

Our conversation went right back to the closing down of the war! We were counting up 'points' that would call our number as to when we would head back to the US. 'OUR SELFISH CONCERNS' we should have gone to the 'radio shack' and reported....and the radio operators would have said; "you're seeing things".

Four to five days had passed and I was down by our docks. "Where did these injured and bodies come from?" I asked. Someone replied, "A ship was sunk and the survivors were in the water for days!" Our 7th Fleet Base was 'a-buzz about our War ending. Our guard was down!

LCI· LANDING CRAFT   864

▲ US troops fighting on Luzon in January. The Japanese under General Tomoyuki Yamashita fought a skilful rearguard campaign in the face of superior forces.

▶ The "Big Three" at Yalta (left to right): Winston Churchill, a sick Franklin D. Roosevelt and Joseph Stalin. The latter agreed to declare war on Japan.

OUR WAR WITH JAPAN WAS COMING TO A CLOSE. A DETACHMENT FROM OUR 33RD WAS ORDERED TO SHANGHAI, CHINA.

WE ASKED WHY?

A government building in Shanghai, China, l ooks much like a Post Office in any city of USA. Chairman MAO TSE TUNG ordered our 01C-"OUT, we do not need you here". Our task Squad was back to SAMAR within 12 days!

DOCKS · SHIPS TOO

10 HOURS ACROSS · CHINA SEA

WANG PO RIVER

BIKES — EVERYWHERE!

DECISIVE WEAPONS

THE BATTLESHIP *YAMATO*

The battleship *Yamato* and her sister ship *Musashi* were built for the Imperial Japanese Navy in the late 1930s and early 1940s under conditions of total secrecy, as the specifications of both vessels breached international treaty limits. Work on the *Yamato* began in November 1937, and she was completed in December 1941. Her combat specifications were impressive. Her main turrets carried nine 18in guns which had a maximum range of 48km (30 miles), and she was armed with forty anti-aircraft guns of various calibres. The *Yamato* also carried six float planes for reconnaissance duties. This 69,088-tonne (68,000-ton) vessel required 2500 officers and men to crew it; yet, with the rising supremacy of naval aviation and submarine warfare, she became an anachronism from the moment she was launched.

Yamato's combat experience bore this out. In early 1944, she was damaged by a submarine torpedo from the USS *Skate*, but she was later able to participate in the Battle of the Philippine Sea. During this action she fired her main armaments, but poor visibility and fast-moving US warships made her contribution negligible. She returned home for re-fitting, and the lessons of the Philippine Sea led to a substantial upgrad-

ing of anti-aircraft armaments. She would have a total of 145 25mm anti-aircraft guns for her final operation, a suicide mission against US invasion forces around Okinawa in April 1945. With enough fuel for only a one-way trip, *Yamato* was spotted by US aircraft well before she reached her destination. An attack by more than 400 US carrier aircraft led to more than 20 bomb and torpedo hits. At 14:20 hours on April 7, her magazine exploded, ripping the ship apart and sending her to the bottom of the Pacific. A total of 2475 crew went down with her.

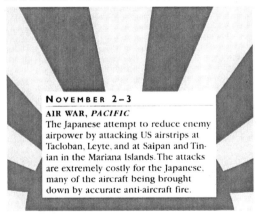

NOVEMBER 2–3

AIR WAR, *PACIFIC*

The Japanese attempt to reduce enemy airpower by attacking US airstrips at Tacloban, Leyte, and at Saipan and Tinian in the Mariana Islands. The attacks are extremely costly for the Japanese, many of the aircraft being brought down by accurate anti-aircraft fire.

KEY PERSONALITIES

EMPEROR HIROHITO

Michinomiya Hirohito (1901–89) was the longest-reigning monarch in Japanese history, taking the throne in 1926 and keeping it until his death in 1989. Although the figurehead of Japanese power, with a quasi-divine status among his people, Hirohito's control over the events that led to war was limited, de facto power residing in the control of the Japanese state by the military establishment. Recent research has shown that Hirohito was actually opposed both to an alliance with Germany and Italy in the Tripartite Pact, and to the Japanese war with the US. Hideki Tojo was the true instigator of the Pacific War, and it was he who rejected a note from President Roosevelt on December 6, 1941, that attempted to avert a conflict.

Hirohito did not believe that Japan could sustain a war against the US, and even in 1942 was urging Tojo to end the conflict. By 1945, Tojo was gone from office and a large number of senior politicians had joined the peace movement. Following the devastation of Hiroshima and Nagasaki by atomic bombs, Hirohito broke with imperial precedent (traditionally, the Emperor is publicly silent) and announced on radio on August 15, 1945 that Japan would accept the US demand for unconditional surrender. In a further step, on January 1, 1946, he announced to the Japanese people that there was no divine status in his office or person. By so doing, and for his role in closing the Japanese resistance, Hirohito managed to escape Allied war crime trials.

The Home Stretch

We came across 'pockets' of forgotten troops of JAPAN! They were non-combative, tired, hungry and confused! (right) one 'Poor-Sole' found living in a cave, OUT BACK! Seemingly, we didn't photograph scenes of the captured, sick or wounded !

One nite this SEABEE had the 'Parameter Watch ' We had 'Swaths' cut around our 'Ritz' Camp Site...with white flags tied to Palm/trees...If the occasion called ...if the white flag went black "Someone is crossing the visual 'fence line'! That nite I did fire.... in the morning exam of the area, a BLACK GOAT invaded the 'sanctuary'! Yes, Many odd happenings to the guards at those times!.

CHRISTMAS EVE 1944 we were 'blacked-out' (lights out at Air-Raid Alert) ! Air-Raids came every nite for months. One `JAP' Plane would enter SAMAR/LEYTE air space every nite. We were parked on our dock beside the Bay... A HOSPITAL SHIP was sitting out in our harbor. A number of wounded men were on that HOSPITAL SHIP. A large RED CROSS was their identification, and well lite also...The 'jap' plane chose the red cross in his sights: The bomb scored within the 'sick bay' and killing! I have the gold bar he wore as a symbol of his pilot qualifications!

The rest of the trip home was beautiful, we were given the privileges of a 'Cruise Ship' lounging and reading, and good food! We all lined the rails as we passed the day long voyage thru the PANAMA CANAL. The first trip of many for this kid...thru the Canal.

FINALLY, arrived Norfolk Virginia, As soon as the dock hands attached the hawsers to the devits, we were ready to get off that ship! We (the 20 of us fought to be first off that gangway!) Not a sole lined the dock...One officer stood by the disembarking ladder,

LC1· LANDING CRAFT 864

▲ US troops fighting on Luzon in January. The Japanese under General Tomoyuki Yamashita fought a skilful rearguard campaign in the face of superior forces.

▶ The "Big Three" at Yalta (left to right): Winston Churchill, a sick Franklin D. Roosevelt and Joseph Stalin. The latter agreed to declare war on Japan.

"What a Motley looking bunch of Guys... Where are your Uniforms?" OUR RESPONSE: "WHAT THE HELLS IT TO YA!" and brushed right past the fellow, that appeared just out of a 90 day officers training course! Next stop was a Shore Patrol desk, asking for our records... "WHAT RECORDS...ALL IN VOICE" Some how I believe those fellows were not about to contest of entry into the USA! WE WERE HOME... WITHOUT ANY WELCOMING FANFARE!

...On to College....55 years later retired in Florida, Living happily on my Golf Cart Chasing the Little 'dimpled' ball, and enjoying this great country of ours....THANKS AGAIN HARRY!

That's All Folks

WENDELL S. ANDERSON

33 RD INDUSTRIAL PARK

'ARROW'...ANDY'S HOME · 33 RD SEABEE BATTALION.

WE MOVED UP FROM THE BEACH! --"DON'T USE YOUR BACK, USE YOUR HEAD!"

'NOT THE RITZ'

TEXICO STATION

OINC ...WHAT'S HIS NAME?

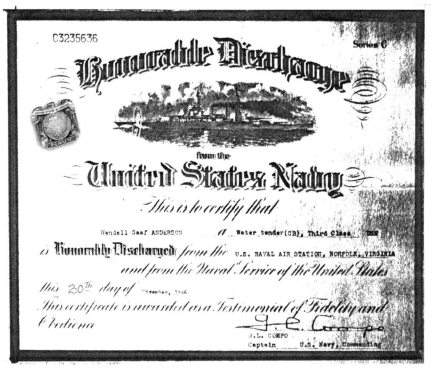

NAVAL HISTORICAL FOUNDATION

Seventy-five years ago, Commodore Dudley Knox wrote in the U.S. Naval Institute Proceedings about the "glaring deficiencies" in collecting and preserving the Navy's written records. Knox's article on "Our Vanishing History and Traditions" give birth to the Naval Historical Foundation in 1926 under the sponsorship of the Secretary of the Navy. From its initial focus on safeguarding the material culture of the Navy, the Foundation has developed into a non-profit organization dedicated to preserving and promoting the full range of naval history. Today, in addition to providing much-needed support to the Navy's historical programs and its flagship United States Navy Museum in Washington, D.C., the Foundation collects oral histories of Navy veterans from World War II through the Cold War, and publishes articles and sponsors symposiums on important naval history topics. To provide increased access by the public to the Navy's historical collections of art, artifacts, documents, and photographs, the Foundation provides historical research and photo reproduction through its Historical Services Division.

CPSIA information can be obtained at www.ICGtesting.com
Printed in the USA
LVOW130141240513

335355LV00004B/8/P

SEABEE

SEABEES "CAN DO!"

The United States Navy

The WWII War-Time Service Career of Wendell S. Anderson

September 1943 thru October 1946

CAREER RETIREE

Wendell S. Anderson

RITZ-CARLTON RESIDENCES
35 Watergate Pl. Res.606
Sarasota Fl. 34236

Home: 941-366-7426
Car Ph: 941-525-4024
Golf cart: 941-320-9680

GÖTLAND

Thank you,
Andy

---

have in hand) is the work of this Combat Veteran and service biography of me; WENDELL S. ANDERSON - (a kid that went [to] war). This publication contains the history of 'ANDY' (my nick-name) and my war time experiences of 1943-1946: the UNITED STATES NAVAL SEABEES.

This book was conceived in these last few years. ...now, in the year of 2013, 70 years 'Post' WORLD WAR II, You may consider me one of your 'Last' eye witness of WW II, and finally bringing these pages and archive to fruition and you.

I have provided my own 'research' compiling data and pictorial items from my personal files. All art work is my own and the photographs are mostly from my files or taken by my 'brownie'. I produced the entire book except for the printing. Printing and binding was done buy PEPPERTREE PRESS of Sarasota, Florida.

I share this book with all that served with me in the 33rd Spec Battalion of U.S. NAVAL SEABEES, as I do not know of any survivors of that 1000 man battalion of World War II. I now share this bit of history and war experiences with you and I would appreciate any comments about this presentation.

Yes, there is COST in this publication ...If you wish to 'cut a check' Payable to: WENDELL S. ANDERSON I will match the fund and pass it along to the three SEABEE MUSEUMS about our country.

GREETINGS

LIFE ... AS IT WAS IN THE 40's ...(you